English Idioms Vocabulary 2022
Complete Edition

Important English Idioms, Sayings, and
Phrases You Should Know to Write and
Speak Like a Well-Educated Native Speaker

by Premier English Learning Publishing

From the Publisher

In this book, we've collected useful English idioms, sayings, and phrases you should know to write and speak like a well-educated native speaker.

This dictionary contains only the most important idioms with clear and simple definitions and up-to-date example sentences.

Study at home, on the road, or in class; bookmark pages; and remember that repetition is the key to memory.

Vocabulary

A good many

Meaning: A lot of.

Dialogue example:

Speaker A: Did anyone enter the building while you were talking?

Speaker B: A good many people I should think.

All hands on deck

Meaning: The phrase is said when there is some kind of emergency, and it requires everyone to work hard; something that takes a lot of effort.

Example: It's been a bit of an all hands on deck effort organizing this meeting.

All hell broke loose

Meaning: A situation that suddenly gets out of control and people start fighting or arguing.

Example: When a fan at a rock concert jumped onto the stage, all hell broke loose.

All walks of life

Meaning: People of all social and economic classes.

Example: In the 19th century, this game was played by all walks of life.

A mile a minute

Meaning: Extremely fast; very rapidly.

Example: My friend talks a mile a minute about his cars.

An awful lot

Meaning: A large amount; very much.

Dialogue example:

Speaker A: Our friend is completely devastated by the death of his parents. What can we do about it?

Speaker B: Not an awful lot, unfortunately.

Any port in a storm

Meaning: To emphasize that in a bad situation you will accept any help or take advantage of any opportunity.

Example: Thanks, Dan! It's not an ideal solution, but hey, any port in a storm.

Article of faith

Meaning: Something you deeply believe in.

Example: This book is an article of faith for her.

As broad as it's long

Meaning: With no significant difference; without any advantage; the same.

Example: Hotel A is a little cheaper, but Hotel B has free breakfast, so it's as broad as it's long.

As drunk as a lord

Meaning: Extremely drunk.

Example: He was as drunk as a lord.

As good a place as any

Meaning: Not perfect, but not worse than any other.

Example: This hotel is as good a place as any to spend the night; It was just as good a place as any to spend the weekend.

As keen as mustard

Meaning: Extremely excited, interested, or enthusiastic.

Example: John got a job at a big company because he was as keen as mustard.

As long as one's arm

Meaning: Extremely long.

Example: My wife owes money to a list of people as long as my arm.

At a low ebb

Meaning: In a state of weakness.

Example: Our economy is at a low ebb; Her health is at a low ebb; My business is now at a low ebb.

At long last

Meaning: Finally; after a long wait.

Example: At long last pizza has arrived; At long last the project was finished.

A torrid time

Meaning: A difficult period filled with problems and challenges.

Example: Our team will definitely face a torrid time in tomorrow's game; I had a torrid time during the championship.

At your earliest convenience

Meaning: As soon as possible.

Example: Please reply to my letter at your earliest convenience.

Avoid something like the plague

Meaning: To avoid something as much as possible.

Example: Rita's been avoiding me like the plague ever since I confessed my love for her.

Back the wrong horse

Meaning: To support something unsuccessful; make the wrong choice or decision.

Example: You really backed the wrong horse when you bought this abandoned house; Despite their vast experience, investors sometimes end up backing the wrong horse.

Barking up the wrong tree

Meaning: Follow the wrong course of action; doing something that will not produce the result you want.

Example: If you expect me to solve all your financial problems, then you, my dear friends, are barking up the wrong tree.

Batten down the hatches

Meaning: To prepare for a difficult or unpleasant situation.

Example: Many companies are battening down the hatches before the crisis.

Be a barrel of fun

Meaning: Be very cheerful, sociable, and enjoyable.

Example: My friend Joe is a real barrel of fun; Festivals are always a barrel of fun.

Be at a loose end

Meaning: Not knowing what to do; have nothing to do.

Example: You can come and help me clean up if you're at a loose end; Get out and take a walk if you're at a loose end.

Beat someone hollow

Meaning: To defeat someone easily and thoroughly.

Example: We scored an incredible 130 points per game and beat that team hollow.

Be beside yourself

Meaning: Being overwhelmed by strong feelings or emotions; unable to think clearly or control oneself.

Example: Tanya was beside herself with grief when her husband died; John was beside himself with excitement.

Be chasing your own tail

Meaning: To do something extremely inefficient or unproductive.

Example: I need to start taking only effective steps towards my goal and stop chasing my own tail.

Bee's knees

Meaning: Excellent; of a very high standard; ideal.

Example: Ron thinks he's the bee's knees; This TV show is the bee's knees; Christmas dinner was just the bee's knees.

Be for the high jump

Meaning: Prepare to be punished; to warn someone that you will punish them if they do something wrong/illegal.

Example: If I catch you stealing, you'll be for the high jump.

Before your very eyes

Meaning: Right in front you; while you are watching.

Example: Thank you for coming to see our magic show! Before your very eyes, I will make this ball disappear.

Beggar belief (or "beggar description")

Meaning: Impossible or not worth believing; impossible to describe or explain.

Example: It almost beggars belief that you completed the project on your own, without any help; Her beauty beggars description!

Be in a tight corner

Meaning: To be in a difficult or tough situation.

Example: With funding being cut, my science project is in a tight corner.

Be in deep water

Meaning: To get into serious trouble.

Example: Having lost all his savings in the casino, he is now in deep water; Sarah has been in deep water since she lost her job.

Be in over your head

Meaning: To be involved in a difficult, dangerous, or unpleasant situation that you cannot handle due to lack of strength, knowledge, or experience.

Dialogue example:

Speaker A: I can beat them all, I have enough resources.

Speaker B: No, you can't! You are in over your head and you know it.

Be in the soup

Meaning: To be in serious trouble.

Example: If Tony and his wife find out what you've done, you'll be in the soup.

Belt and braces

Meaning: Do some extra actions to make sure something is safe; providing double security.

Example: I have a very important meeting tomorrow, so I set an alarm on my phone, tablet, and watch - belt and braces, I admit.

Be on the best of terms with someone (or "be on good terms")

Meaning: To have a good/excellent relationship with someone.

Dialogue example:

Speaker A: Do you think Dan will agree to hire me?

Speaker B: I'm not on the best of terms with Dan at the moment, so you'll have to ask him yourself.

Be on tenterhooks

Meaning: Very nervous, excited, and thrilled because you are wondering what is going to happen in a specific situation.

Example: We were on tenterhooks all evening waiting for the big news; I've been on tenterhooks all month, waiting for the DNA test results.

Be on the cusp of

Meaning: To be at the time when a situation/condition is going to change.

Example: We're on the very cusp of the new world.

Be on the skids

Meaning: To be in a difficult or bad situation.

Example: Their family business seems to be on the skids.

Between the devil and the deep blue sea

Meaning: In a bad situation with two equally unpleasant options.

Example: With all my debts, I'm really between the devil and the deep blue sea, because I need to sell either my house or business.

Blot on something

Meaning: A fault or mistake that ruins someone's reputation; something that spoils something.

Example: A serious blot on my career; This incident is a blot on our family name.

Blow something or someone out of the water

Meaning: Completely destroy, ruin, or defeat someone/something.

Example: These terrible reviews from the critics will blow my restaurant out of the water.

Bone of contention

Meaning: Something that people argue about; subject of a disagreement.

Example: The main bone of contention between us is money.

Bring something to the table

Meaning: To contribute; to provide something useful to others in your group; bring up for discussion.

Example: Our new worker will bring many important skills to the table; So, John, what are you going to bring to the table besides your vast experience?

Burn the midnight oil

Meaning: To work/read/study late into the night.

Example: I have to burn the midnight oil to finish my homework.

Bursting at the seams

Meaning: Extremely full or crowded.

Example: When the whole family comes home for Christmas, our house is bursting at the seams.

Burst someone's bubble

Meaning: To end someone's illusions, dreams, beliefs, or hopes by telling them the truth.

Example: I don't want to burst your bubble, but she's gone and won't come back to you.

By jove

Meaning: To emphasize that you are very surprised or excited.

Dialogue example:

Speaker A: Thank you for your testimony, sir. But before we let you go, there's one more thing I need to do.

Speaker B: What exactly?

Speaker A: I will take your fingerprints and a hair sample.

Speaker B: Will you, by jove? Well, get on with it then!

By leaps and bounds

Meaning: Extremely fast.

Example: His English is improving by leaps and bounds; Her admiration for him was growing by leaps and bounds.

By the look of things/it

Meaning: Based on the information you have at the moment.

Example: By the look of things, he did not commit a crime; Prices are going to go up, by the look of it.

Call a spade a spade

Meaning: Speak directly and clearly about something, even if it is unpleasant.

Example: Let's call a spade a spade - you cheated on me with my best friend!

Cannot do something for toffee

Meaning: Be very incompetent and extremely bad at something.

Example: I can't drive a truck for toffee; I can't sing for toffee.

Can't make head nor tail of something

Meaning: Can't understand something at all.

Example: I couldn't make head nor tail of that old book.

Carved in stone

Meaning: Cannot be changed; permanent.

Example: You can pitch us your ideas about our product, we haven't carved anything in stone yet.

Cast a shadow over/on

Meaning: To make a situation less encouraging, enjoyable, or hopeful and more unpleasant.

Example: The sad news about his health condition cast a shadow over our meeting.

Catch someone red-handed

Meaning: To discover (or catch) someone in the act of committing a crime or doing something bad or illegal.

Example: Finn was caught red-handed in a robbery; The police caught her red-handed with stolen diamonds in her purse.

Cat got your tongue?

Meaning: To emphasize that someone is unusually quiet.

Dialogue example:

Speaker A: You have lipstick marks on your neck. Who is she?

Speaker B: Ohhh.

Speaker A: What's the matter? Cat got your tongue?

Champagne tastes, beer wages (or "champagne taste on a beer budget")

Meaning: Someone with expensive preferences and low income.

Example: Tina spent her entire salary on a designer jacket, she definitely has champagne taste on a beer budget.

Clip someone's wings

Meaning: To limit someone's power, freedom, or comfort.

Example: Her parents clipped her wings by refusing to pay for her luxurious life.

Close the door/stable door after the horse has bolted

Meaning: To emphasize that it is too late to take action to prevent something undesirable/unwanted from happening, because it has already happened.

Dialogue example:

Speaker A: Hello sir! We would like to offer you a free alarm system for your store.

Speaker B: Thanks for the offer, but I've already been robbed, so it's a bit late to close the door after the horse has bolted.

Come a cropper

Meaning: To fail badly; to fall down.

Example: Investors have come a cropper on this project; Dan came a cropper on the ski slopes and broke his arm.

Come from behind

Meaning: To win unexpectedly while in a losing position.

Example: The red team came from behind to beat the green team 6-5.

Cook someone's goose

Meaning: To ruin someone's plans; prevent success.

Example: This front-page scandal news will surely cook his goose.

Cook the books

Meaning: To falsify a company's financial records.

Example: He made thousands from cooking the books before the fraud department caught him.

Couldn't fight their way out of a paper bag

Meaning: Weak or ineffective; without much energy or ability.

Example: He's absolutely useless as an ally - he couldn't fight his way out of a paper bag!

Counsel of despair

Meaning: An admission of defeat or failure.

Example: It is sad to hear such a counsel of despair from our government about the situation with our economy.

Crawl out of the woodwork

Meaning: To suddenly or unexpectedly appear after a long time (usually for selfish purposes).

Example: After his song became a number one hit, his ex-girlfriend came crawling out of the woodwork.

Cry for the moon

Meaning: To wish for something unattainable.

Dialogue example:

Speaker A: I do not have time for anything. I wish there were at least 40 hours in a day.

Speaker B: Well, you're crying for the moon!

Cute as a button

Meaning: Adorable; graceful; very cute.

Example: Your little sister is cute as a button.

Cut short

Meaning: To end something earlier than expected or planned.

Example: He was a promising surgeon, but his career was cut short by a terrible accident with his left hand.

Cut something to the bone

Meaning: To cut down severely; reduce to the bare minimum.

Example: We need to cut our expenses to the bone.

Die in vain

Meaning: To die for nothing; to sacrifice yourself for a cause that ends up being useless.

Example: Commander, you need to retreat! Don't let your warriors die in vain.

Dig one's heels in

Meaning: To emphasize that you do not want to change your plans; to refuse to do something.

Example: I tried to persuade her to choose another restaurant, but she dug her heels in.

Discretion is the better part of valour

Meaning: To emphasize that it is better to avoid unnecessary risks or unpleasant situations.

Example: Danny, my boy, discretion is the better part of valour, so don't be a hero and go home!

Dock someone's wages

Meaning: To reduce the amount of money you pay someone as a penalty/punishment.

Dialogue example:

Speaker A: Boss, John delivered the package, but it's damaged. Should I accept it and pay him?

Speaker B: Fine, but dock his wages.

Don't give up the day job

Meaning: Make it clear to someone that you do not believe in the success of their new idea, plan, project, or hobby (in a playful and non-offensive manner).

Dialogue example:

Speaker A: What do you think of my new book idea?

Speaker B: Hmm, interesting idea, but don't give up the day job.

Do someone a world of good

Meaning: To make someone feel better or much healthier; to be very helpful for someone.

Example: The mountain air will do you a world of good.

Down in the dumps

Meaning: Extremely sad; unhappy; very depressed.

Example: Vince has been down in the dumps ever since his wife died.

Dress in layers

Meaning: Dress warmly; wear several types of clothing at once to keep warm.

Example: You're going to Norway, so dress in layers.

Drop a clanger

Meaning: To say or do something foolish or embarrassing.

Example: I dropped a clanger when I asked him about the wedding on our first date.

Easy on the eye/ear

Meaning: Pleasant to look at or listen to.

Example: I painted my bedroom in pastel colours to make it easy on the eye; I like classical music because it's easy on the ear.

Eat someone out of house and home

Meaning: To eat a lot of someone's food, especially when you're a guest in their house (often said in a humorous manner).

Example: Aunt Lucy, Uncle John, I didn't invite you here to eat me out of house and home.

Educated guess

Meaning: An assumption based on knowledge of the situation and therefore most likely correct.

Example: As a mechanic, I can't say exactly how much it will cost to repair your car, but I can make an educated guess.

Every dog has its day

Meaning: Everyone has at least one happy or successful moment in life.

Example: Your startup has failed, but don't lose hope and remember that every dog has its day.

Fall by the wayside

Meaning: To fail to finish an activity; no longer be effective.

Example: Many clubs and resorts fall by the wayside during a recession.

Fall into the wrong hands

Meaning: To be discovered by your enemy; to be discovered by unfriendly/dangerous people.

Example: If this document falls into the wrong hands, then it could be catastrophic.

Fat chance

Meaning: Not likely to happen; extremely unlikely.

Example: Let's face it, you have a fat chance of getting the job; Fat chance we can get there on time.

Faux pas

Meaning: A social mistake; embarrassing error; something socially awkward.

Example: Arriving at the party early or on time is a faux pas.

Fit to drop

Meaning: Very tired.

Example: After the marathon we were fit to drop.

Flatter to deceive

Meaning: Looks promising at first glance, but ends up being very disappointing.

Example: As with most new investment companies, their early success flattered to deceive.

Flog/beat a dead horse

Meaning: To keep wasting energy or time on something when there is no chance of success.

Dialogue example:

Speaker A: Stop asking me these questions, I won't tell you anyway.

Speaker B: But I need answers. Tell me everything you know!

Speaker A: You do like flogging a dead horse, don't you?

Fly off the handle

Meaning: To become very angry; to lose control; react too angrily to something insignificant.

Example: I'm sorry I unintentionally pushed your girlfriend, but there's no need to fly off the handle.

For donkey's years

Meaning: For a very long time.

Example: I've had this ring for donkey's years; The new railway won't be ready for donkey's years.

For want of a better word/term

Meaning: Lacking a more precise word/term; to emphasize that you cannot think of a more accurate way of explaining what you mean.

Example: He is, for want of a better word, a grumbler; She should behave more respectfully or, for want of a better word, decently.

Friends in high places

Meaning: Influential and powerful people who will help you in case of emergency.

Example: I have plenty of friends in high places, so finding a new job is not a problem.

Get a grip on yourself

Meaning: To make an effort to control your behaviour, manners, or emotions.

Example: Get a grip on yourself and stop crying!

Get your hands on someone

Meaning: To catch or find someone.

Example: When I get my hands on him, he will have to pay off his debts.

Give someone the runaround

Meaning: To delay someone by providing useless information or directions.

Dialogue example:

Speaker A: When do you plan to launch the project?

Speaker B: On Monday or Wednesday. Maybe Saturday. Or maybe a week from now.

Speaker A: Sounds like you're giving me the runaround. I need to know exactly when this project will be launched!

Go at it hammer and tongs

Meaning: With great energy, power, passion, or enthusiasm; very intensively; to have a very noisy argument.

Example: Our neighbors were going at it hammer and tongs all night.

Go down like a lead balloon

Meaning: To be extremely unsuccessful, unloved, or unpopular.

Example: His political joke went down like a lead balloon; These stupid questions go down like a lead balloon.

Go down like ninepins

Meaning: To be damaged in large numbers; when a lot of people suddenly become ill.

Example: Trees and road signs were going down like ninepins in a storm.

Go easy on someone

Meaning: To treat someone more gently, less harshly.

Example: Go easy on your son, he's just a kid.

Go off-book

Meaning: To not follow the script; disturb the order of things.

Dialogue example:

Speaker A: I have an idea! Let's take half of Mike's share for ourselves.

Speaker B: I have a better idea! Let's split the money between the three of us and leave Mike aside.

Speaker C: Stop arguing! Let's stick to the plan. I don't like it when you two go off-book like this.

Go off the rails

Meaning: Start behaving in an uncontrollable or intolerable way.

Example: My daughter started going off the rails shortly after graduation.

Go the extra mile

Meaning: To make an extra effort; do more than is expected of you.

Example: We need to go the extra mile to release the game on time.

Go through the floor

Meaning: To fall to an ultra-low level.

Example: Due to the crisis, resort prices have gone through the floor.

Guard your tongue

Meaning: Being very careful about what you say.

Example: Guard your tongue, woman, you're talking about my mother!

Hang in the balance

Meaning: Not yet decided; unsure of the future; not certain what will happen to it.

Example: After that scandal, the future of my company still hangs in the balance.

Have a bone to pick with someone

Meaning: To talk to the person about the things that annoy you; to have an issue to discuss or argue about.

Example: Darling, I've got a bone to pick with you. Why did you decide to have dinner with your ex-boyfriend again?

Have a bee in your bonnet

Meaning: To talk a lot about something or be extremely passionate about it (mostly in a very annoying way).

Example: He's got a bee in his bonnet about video games.

Have another string to one's bow

Meaning: To emphasize that you have another plan/idea/skill to use if it's needed.

Example: You're right, my plan didn't work, but I have another string to my bow.

Have a short fuse

Meaning: To get angry/mad very easily.

Example: Her boss is known to have a short fuse.

Have bigger fish to fry

Meaning: Have more important things to do.

Dialogue example:

Speaker A: Could you help me with my project?

Speaker B: Sorry, I've got bigger fish to fry!

Have feet of clay

Meaning: To have hidden flaws or weaknesses.

Example: Most of the greatest minds in history had feet of clay; Fans don't want to see their idols with feet of clay.

Have it in you

Meaning: To have a certain quality/skill.

Example: You don't have it in you to make the difficult choices.

Have one's blood up

Meaning: To be angry or inflamed; to be in an aggressive or violent mood.

Example: Her offensive jokes really got my blood up.

Have the stomach for something

Meaning: To have enough determination to do something difficult, risky, or unpleasant.

Example: I don't have the stomach for a real fight; I have no stomach for horror movies.

Have your back to the wall

Meaning: Find yourself in an extremely difficult situation with limited options for action.

Example: He really has his back to the wall because of all his debts and loans.

Have your fair share of something

Meaning: A lot or more than enough of something.

Example: Listen to me Jonny, I've done my fair share of travelling and I'm telling you the most delicious desserts can be found in Norway; He's had his fair share of failures in his life.

Hold sway

Meaning: To have a great influence on someone's opinion or behaviour; to control someone/something.

Example: His warriors hold sway over much of the continent; Traditional values still hold sway in our home.

Hot on the trail of

Meaning: Close to catching someone; close to finding something.

Example: A detective is hot on the trail of a murder; Recruiters are hot on the trail of young soccer stars.

Hot under the collar

Meaning: Extremely angry or embarrassed.

Example: I got really hot under the collar when my ex-girlfriend showed up at the party.

If all else fails

Meaning: If all other attempts have failed; if what was planned cannot happen.

Dialogue example:

Speaker A: You look gorgeous! You've always been so stylish and unique in your outfits.

Speaker B: Thanks! If all else fails, I can get into the fashion business.

In a bind

Meaning: To be in a difficult, tough, or threatening situation.

Example: I'm in a bind to pay my bills; This new schedule has put me in a bind.

In a stew

Meaning: Worried; confused; upset.

Example: Jennifer is all in a stew over her lost mobile phone.

In cold blood

Meaning: In an unemotional way; in a cruel and calm way.

Example: She shot him in cold blood.

In fits and starts

Meaning: Not stable; not smooth; often stops and then starts again.

Example: The music player works in fits and starts.

In full swing

Meaning: At the peak of activity.

Example: When my girlfriend and I arrived, the party was in full swing.

In one piece

Meaning: Unscathed; without being damaged.

Dialogue example:

Speaker A: Ouch, an icicle just fell on me.

Speaker B: You in one piece?

Speaker A: And still breathing, thanks.

In someone's bad books

Meaning: In someone's disfavour.

Example: I'm in her bad books at the moment because I forgot to buy her a birthday present.

In store for someone

Meaning: Forthcoming; about to happen to someone; planned for someone.

Example: I have a big surprise in store for you.

In the fullness of time

Meaning: Eventually; after a long time.

Example: I'm sure she'll forgive me everything in the fullness of time; All her secrets will be revealed in the fullness of time.

In words of one syllable

Meaning: In clear and simple language without complicated words and expressions.

Example: Please explain this theorem to me in words of one syllable; Could you repeat your speech in words of one syllable?

Itching to do something

Meaning: Being extremely impatient because you want to do/get something as soon as possible.

Example: She's itching to go to college; He's itching to get back to work.

It's high time

Meaning: To emphasize that it's time to do what should have been done a long time ago.

Example: It's high time you realize that you're a father; It's high time you got a job.

It's no skin off my nose

Meaning: To emphasize that you don't care if someone does something, because it's not your responsibility.

Dialogue example:

Speaker A: They will stop working with us if we do not fulfil all the terms of the contract.

Speaker B: It's no skin off my nose, I'm just a trainee in this company.

Jog someone's memory

Meaning: To refresh someone's memory; to help someone remember something.

Example: His old diary jogged his memory; That family photo jogged my memory.

Jumping-off point

Meaning: A starting point for an activity, journey, or project.

Example: Amsterdam is the best jumping-off point for a trip to the Netherlands.

Jumping on shadows

Meaning: Being intensely frightened by things that shouldn't normally frighten you.

Example: Ever since she returned from the expedition, she's been acting strangely - jumping on shadows, constantly checking if the front door is closed.

Keep a low profile (or "keep the spotlight off")

Meaning: To avoid attracting attention.

Example: I hope you will try to keep a low profile tonight. Don't forget that the police are looking for you.

Keep one's chin up

Meaning: To stay cheerful during difficult or challenging times.

Dialogue example:

Speaker A: Don't worry so much about bad test results, you'll retake them in a month and get the highest possible score. I believe in you!

Speaker B: I'll try my best to keep my chin up, thanks dad.

Keep one's nose to the grindstone

Meaning: To do intensive, heavy, or continuous work.

Example: Dina's got to keep her nose to the grindstone to feed her family.

Keep one's powder dry

Meaning: To remain calm and be fully prepared for a particular situation/event.

Example: Conflict may not arise, but there is no harm in keeping your powder dry.

Keep one's eyes peeled

Meaning: To watch very carefully.

Example: Just drive slowly and keep your eyes peeled.

Keep one's hair on

Meaning: To urge someone not to panic and stay calm.

Example: Keep your hair on, we're almost there!

Keep tabs on

Meaning: To watch someone/something carefully; always know where someone/something is.

Dialogue example:

Speaker A: Where is Jimmy?

Speaker B: How should I know? I don't keep tabs on him.

Kill or cure

Meaning: Either success or total failure.

Example: This project will be kill or cure for our company; This discovery will kill or cure our research.

Know something by heart

Meaning: To memorize something completely.

Example: I'm pretty sure I know this song by heart.

Labour the point

Meaning: Keep talking or pitching your idea/plan in a boring or annoying manner.

Example: I don't want to labour the point, but you should know that my project is much better.

Lead someone a merry dance

Meaning: To treat someone unfairly or badly over period of time; to cause a lot of problems.

Example: She led me a merry dance before I finally got her to sign the divorce papers.

Lead someone down the garden path

Meaning: To mislead; cheat; deceive.

Example: Vince may have led me down the garden path with that investment opportunity.

Leap in the dark

Meaning: An action performed without the certainty of what will happen as a result.

Example: It would be a leap in the dark to start a company without testing your product; My move to Europe was a leap in the dark.

Leave in the lurch

Meaning: To leave/abandon someone at a time when they really need your assistance or support.

Example: My colleagues left me in the lurch and I had to finish the report myself.

Leave no stone unturned

Meaning: To do everything you can to find something.

Example: Ginny left no stone unturned in her search for her real parents.

Lend an ear

Meaning: To listen to someone in a friendly and sympathetic manner.

Example: Could you please lend me your ear for a minute? I have a confession to make; My friends are always ready to lend an ear to me.

Lie low

Meaning: To remain hidden; to try not to be seen or noticed.

Example: After the last fraud, the scammers decided to lie low for a while.

Load the dice against someone

Meaning: To put someone at a disadvantage.

Example: Lack of experience loaded the dice against Sarrah as a candidate for the position.

Long shot

Meaning: With very little chance of success.

Example: It's a long shot, but I still want to try to get the job.

Loosen someone's tongue

Meaning: To make someone speak more openly or freely.

Example: The beer had loosened John's tongue.

Lose one's bottle

Meaning: To lose one's nerve or courage in a stressful situation.

Example: I wanted to fight him back, but I lost my bottle at the last minute.

Magic touch

Meaning: The ability to do something extremely well.

Example: He has a magic touch in the kitchen; Dan seems to have a magic touch with cars.

Make a meal of something (or "make a big deal of something")

Meaning: To treat something in a way that makes it seem more significant, valuable, or important than it actually is.

Example: Students always make such a meal of the simplest test; He made such a meal of that task - it only took him half an hour!

Make a rod for your own back

Meaning: To do something that will cause you trouble/problems in the future.

Example: Our management made a rod for their own back when they fired all the highly skilled workers.

Move heaven and earth

Meaning: To try as hard as you can to achieve something; to stop at nothing.

Example: I had to move heaven and earth to get my dream job.

Nip something in the bud

Meaning: To stop something at an early stage before it becomes a big problem.

Example: It is extremely important to nip this problem in the bud.

Nod is as good as a wink

Meaning: To emphasize that there is no need to explain something further, because the person already understands or knows enough about it.

Dialogue example:

Speaker A: Do you know why Tanya is so upset?

Speaker B: All I know is that she met her ex-boyfriend at the supermarket.

Speaker A: Come on, a nod is as good as a wink. It's all because of him.

No holds barred

Meaning: Without any restrictions or limits.

Example: In my house you can do whatever you want, no holds barred.

No picnic

Meaning: Quite difficult or unpleasant.

Example: College life is no picnic; Being a single parent is no picnic.

No prizes for guessing

Meaning: To emphasize that it is very easy to guess something; something that is very obvious.

Example: No prizes for guessing where John is; No prizes for guessing the answer to that simple question.

Not a bed of roses

Meaning: Having some unpleasant aspects.

Example: My job is not a bed of roses.

Not a hair out of place

Meaning: To have a very neat/tidy appearance.

Example: He was so gorgeous in his new suit, not a hair out of place; She was splendidly dressed, not a hair out of place.

Not budge an inch

Meaning: To refuse to change your mind/position.

Example: I tried to negotiate a better offer but they wouldn't budge an inch.

Not have a care in the world

Meaning: Without worrying about anything.

Example: I miss the old school days, when I didn't have a care in the world.

Not have a leg to stand on

Meaning: To have no proof of your rightness/correctness.

Dialogue example:

Speaker A: What is your evidence?

Speaker B: I don't have a leg to stand on. It's only my word against hers.

Not in one's right mind

Meaning: Mentally ill; cannot think clearly.

Example: Leave her alone, she's not in her right mind; I know he's scared to death, but I need him in his right mind!

Not best pleased

Meaning: Annoyed; irritated; angry; unhappy.

Example: I wasn't best pleased when my mother married again; and so soon after my father's death!

No two ways about it

Meaning: Definitely; for sure; without a doubt.

Example: If you leave me here alone and go drink beer with your friends, I'll break up with you! No two ways about it!

Off one's hands

Meaning: Removed from one's responsibility; no longer needing to be looked after.

Example: If you are unable to complete these tasks, I'll be glad to take them off your hands.

Off the mark

Meaning: Not correct; inaccurate; wrong ("on the mark" - correct/right).

Example: Your remark is off the mark; The facts she provided are way off the mark.

Of the essence

Meaning: Absolutely necessary in a particular situation.

Example: Speed is of the essence in dealing with an emergency; We must hurry, time is of the essence!

On a hiding to nothing

Meaning: Without the slightest chance of success; sure to fail.

Example: He's on a hiding to nothing in this competition.

One for the books

Meaning: Very surprising or unexpected.

Example: His last-minute goal was one for the books.

On speaking terms

Meaning: Amicable or friendly enough to talk (often used in negative form).

Example: I'm not on speaking terms with my family; I don't know how after all his intrigues and betrayals she's somehow still on speaking terms with him; We're on speaking terms with John, but I wouldn't say we're real friends.

On the loose

Meaning: A dangerous animal/criminal who walks free (mostly because they have escaped from prison/cage).

Example: He's still on the loose - but not for long. The police have already blocked all exits from the city.

On the verge of something (or "on the brink of something")

Meaning: Very close to experiencing something; the moment when something is about to happen.

Example: We are on the verge of a big discovery; We stand on a brink of a great change.

On your own head be it

Meaning: To warn someone that they will have to take full responsibility for what they are about to do.

Example: If you choose to disobey my order, then on your own heads be it!

Out of sorts

Meaning: Slightly ill/unwell/unhappy.

Example: He's feeling a bit out of sorts.

Out of the corner of one's eye

Meaning: Looking at something indirectly; when you see something briefly, rather than clearly.

Example: Out of the corner of my eye, I saw my wife talking to some stranger.

Over the hill

Meaning: No longer young and fit; too old to perform as well as before.

Example: Ron is over the hill as a professional basketball player.

Pale into insignificance

Meaning: To appear less important, significant, or impressive when compared with something else.

Example: All my problems pale into insignificance when compared to the problems of the homeless.

Paragon of virtue

Meaning: One who has perfect moral values.

Example: Ron was considered to be a paragon of virtue; I don't expect any billionaire to be a paragon of virtue.

Pass the buck

Meaning: To shift the responsibility to someone else.

Example: It's your fault because you're in charge, so don't try to pass the buck.

Perish the thought

Meaning: To emphasize that the proposed idea/concept/plan is ridiculous and unlikely to be implemented.

Example: I will never marry her - perish the thought!

Pipe dream

Meaning: Something that is not destined to come true.

Example: His plans to become president of several countries at once are simply pipe dreams.

Plain sailing

Meaning: Without problems; smooth; easy.

Example: Her surgery was plain sailing; Pregnancy wasn't all plain sailing.

Play into someone's hands

Meaning: To do something that will be to your disadvantage and to your opponent's advantage; to act in the way your opponent wants you to act.

Example: It would be playing into Rita's hands to react to her humiliating jokes.

Play your cards right

Meaning: To behave in a way that is beneficial in a given situation; to do something in a well-planned way.

Example: If you play your cards right, you can win this competition.

Pull out all the stops

Meaning: To make every possible effort; do the best you can.

Example: The police pulled out all the stops to find the robber; Dan pulled out all the stops to finish the project on time.

Pull someone's leg

Meaning: To tell someone a lie, as a joke.

Example: Calm down Ian, it's not true, I was only pulling your leg.

Pull the plug

Meaning: To prevent further activity; to prevent something from continuing.

Example: I have enough power to pull the plug on your career; She decided to pull the plug on her research.

Put it down to experience

Meaning: To regard a bad, difficult, or unpleasant situation as a learning experience rather than a punishment.

Example: Everyone makes mistakes, don't worry so much and put it down to experience.

Put someone wise to something

Meaning: To clarify something for someone; to tell someone about something.

Example: I showed up at the appointed time. Tommy put me wise to the situation and we started negotiations.

Put something to bed

Meaning: To successfully deal with something; to finish work on something.

Example: Before putting the agreement to bed, we must clarify a few clauses; Let's just put the issue to bed and stop arguing!

Put the cart before the horse

Meaning: To do something in the wrong order.

Example: Aren't you putting the cart before the horse by choosing a wedding venue before the actual proposal?

Raining cats and dogs

Meaning: Heavy rain.

Example: Better stay at home, it's raining cats and dogs outside.

Rain on someone's parade

Meaning: To do something that ruins someone's plans; dampen one's excitement.

Example: I hate to rain on your parade, but I think your name on the list of finalists is just a typo. You took 25th place, not third, sorry.

Ride for a fall

Meaning: To do something unwise and reckless that will lead to failure or injury.

Example: Nina's riding for a fall with the dubious investments she's been making lately.

Rob someone blind

Meaning: To cheat someone and take their money; to steal everything someone owns.

Dialogue example:

Speaker A: Hello madam! Would you like to multiply your savings? For just a thousand pounds, I can tell you how to do it.

Speaker B: You are trying to rob me blind. I won't buy it!

Rocky road

Meaning: A difficult/challenging period.

Example: The rocky road to the championship.

Rub shoulders/elbows with

Meaning: To spend time with someone.

Example: She loves rubbing shoulders with the rich and famous.

Rue the day

Meaning: To curse or bitterly regret a moment in your life; to be very sorry for something.

Example: I rue the day I lost my wife; When I find him, he'll rue the day he was born!

Said the pot to the kettle (or "the pot calling the kettle black")

Meaning: A witty remark to someone who says something bad/insulting about another person, when they themselves are guilty of the same thing.

Dialogue example:

Speaker A: He is so arrogant and selfish!

Speaker B: Said the pot to the kettle.

Sail close to the wind

Meaning: To do something dangerous, risky, illegal, or unacceptable.

Example: Illegal tobacco company was sailing close to the wind.

Salt something away

Meaning: To save something for later.

Example: Don't worry about the wedding expenses, I have fifty thousand pounds salted away for that.

Say your piece

Meaning: To state your opinion; to say what you want to say.

Example: Stop glaring at us! Just say your piece about the incident.

See fit

Meaning: To consider proper or desirable.

Example: When you find this fraudster, deal with him however you see fit.

See the light of day

Meaning: To come into existence; first time to appear.

Example: This video game first saw the light of day in 2005.

Serve someone right

Meaning: To emphasize that someone deserves all the bad things that happen to them.

Dialogue example:

Speaker A: He is in trouble with the law again.

Speaker B: It serves him right!

Set someone's mind at ease

Meaning: Help someone to calm down/stop worrying.

Example: He could set her mind at ease by telling her the truth.

Set something in motion

Meaning: To start a process/series of events.

Example: By not taking their money, you set the bankruptcy in motion.

Settle a score

Meaning: To punish or harm someone for something bad that they did to you in the past; take revenge; pay the debt off.

Dialogue example:

Speaker A: Will you join us to fight the hooligans from 15th Street?

Speaker B: Yes, I have some scores to settle with them.

Shadow of one's former self

Meaning: Not as good, powerful, or capable as before.

Example: Three years after her injury, she returned to the basketball court, but was only a shadow of her former self.

Shed some light

Meaning: To provide additional/missing information about something.

Example: Hopefully these documents will shed some light on her past.

Sitting duck

Meaning: Easy target; someone who is very easy for the enemy to attack.

Example: Without body armor and a helmet, I'm a sitting duck for the enemy; children are often sitting ducks for scammers.

Sitting pretty

Meaning: To be in a good, comfortable, privileged, or favored position.

Example: Cariba really is sitting pretty with her new job as CEO; With profits up 200 percent, my company is sitting pretty.

Slip of the tongue

Meaning: Something that was said by accident/mistakenly.

Example: Did I call you Rachel? It must have been a slip of the tongue.

Small wonder

Meaning: Not surprising.

Example: It's small wonder he wanted me back, I'm the best girlfriend on a planet; It's small wonder the kids are bored.

Smarten up your act

Meaning: To improve your behavior; make more of an effort.

Example: Tell your king that he'll have to smarten up his act if he needs me as an ally.

Someone's lot in life

Meaning: General state of life; general situation in life.

Example: John seems happy enough with his lot in life; He tried to accept the bankruptcy of his company as his lot in life, but he could not.

Splinter off from something

Meaning: To separate from the greater part of something; to separate from a larger group.

Example: Small group splintered off from main camp.

Squeeze something out of someone

Meaning: To force someone to do or give something (mostly information).

Example: It's just a shame we couldn't squeeze anything out of Dan and his accomplices. They probably could have told us some interesting things about the robbery!

Stand your ground (or "hold your ground")

Meaning: To refuse to change your opinion; continue to support a particular position or point of view in an argument; to stay where you are when someone threatens or intimidates you.

Example: Our meeting was unsuccessful because Harry stood his ground and refused to accept any of our offers; The hooligans threatened him, but John stood his ground.

Stem the tide

Meaning: To stop the growth or continuation of something.

Example: These strict measures are designed to stem the tide of illegal immigration.

Straight from the horse's mouth

Meaning: To hear information from someone who knows for sure that it's true (mainly because that person has personally seen or heard something that confirms the accuracy of the information).

Example: Oh, you're here! John already told me what's been happening, but I'd like to hear it straight from the horse's mouth.

Strain every nerve

Meaning: To make every possible effort; do the best you can.

Example: I will strain every nerve to finish the book.

Sure as eggs is eggs

Meaning: Without any doubt; for certain.

Dialogue example:

Speaker A: Are you sure you are pregnant?

Speaker B: Sure as eggs is eggs!

Sweep something under the carpet

Meaning: To deliberately ignore a problem/issue in the hope that it will be overlooked or forgotten.

Example: You can't just sweep your financial problems under the carpet.

Sweep the board

Meaning: To win everything possible.

Example: My team swept the board in the boxing competition.

Take a hint

Meaning: To understand something that is suggested or offered to you indirectly.

Dialogue example:

Speaker A: Nancy, would you like to have dinner with me tonight?

Speaker B: I'd love to, but I have a lot of work to do. And besides, my knee hurts. So, uh...

Speaker A: Okay, I can take a hint.

Take it from me

Meaning: To emphasize that you are absolutely sure of what you are saying.

Dialogue example:

Speaker A: What is your opinion of John?

Speaker B: You can take it from me, he's a wonderful man.

Take matters into your own hands

Meaning: To do something yourself because others have refused or failed.

Example: We failed his order to eliminate the target. So he took matters into his own hands and killed the target.

Take something as read

Meaning: To agree/accept that something is true without any evidence.

Example: We took it as read that he was a spy; Let's take it as a read that he was the first to invent this method.

Take the bull by the horns

Meaning: To confidently deal with a dangerous or difficult situation.

Example: I know that you are a very empathetic person, but it's time to take the bull by the horns and fire inefficient employees.

Tall order

Meaning: A request or task that is extremely difficult to complete.

Example: Completing this task on time was a tall order, but we did it; Spending more time with kids is a tall order for busy parents.

Thank your lucky stars

Meaning: To be extremely grateful.

Example: You should thank your lucky stars that you managed to survive the accident.

That's one way of putting it

Meaning: To emphasize that someone said something completely different from the intended meaning of their words (mostly in a sarcastic or flirty manner).

Dialogue example:

Speaker A: You look really hot!

Speaker B: Well, that's one way of putting it.

The jury is still out

Meaning: To emphasize that something has not yet been decided/answered.

Example: The jury is still out on whether red wine can be good for you.

The lion's share

Meaning: Bigger half; largest part.

Example: I spend the lion's share of my salary on rent.

The mists of time/history

Meaning: To emphasize that something happened so long ago that you barely remember it.

Example: The answer is lost in the mists of time; The origins of this phrase are lost in the mists of history/time.

The more the merrier

Meaning: To emphasize that more people will make the event or activity more enjoyable.

Dialogue example:

Speaker A: Can I bring my brother to your birthday party?

Speaker B: Sure, the more the merrier!

There's no telling

Meaning: Impossible to know for sure.

Example: If he fails in negotiations, there's no telling how many people will lose their jobs.

There's no time like the present

Meaning: To emphasize that now is the best time to do something.

Dialogue example:

Speaker A: When would you like to meet?

Speaker B: There's no time like the present. See you in an hour at our favourite cafe.

There's safety in numbers

Meaning: To emphasize that when you are in a large group with other people, you are less likely to be harmed.

Dialogue example:

Speaker A: We are lost in the woods at night. What should we do?

Speaker B: We must stick together. There's safety in numbers.

The worse for wear

Meaning: Exhausted; tired; in poor condition; beaten up from use.

Example: He was slightly the worse for wear after a grueling workout; Your jacket seems to be the worse for wear - I'll buy you a new one.

Throw a spanner in the works

Meaning: To prevent things from going as planned (mainly by causing problems or difficulties).

Example: I was ready to publish my novel when my little sister threw a spanner in the works by deleting the book from my computer.

Throw cold water on something

Meaning: To destroy someone's enthusiasm for something; be extremely pessimistic about someone's plans or ideas.

Example: You're always throwing cold water on my ideas!

Tie up loose ends

Meaning: To deal with little issues/problems left unresolved from something; to complete minor matters that are the result of a previous action.

Example: It was almost a perfect heist. With all the witnesses under control, all that remained was to tie up loose ends.

Till the cows come home

Meaning: For a long period of time.

Example: You can convince me till the cows come home, but I won't change my mind.

To someone's liking

Meaning: Fitting someone's preferences; enjoyable to someone.

Dialogue example:

Speaker A: Everything to your liking, thus far?

Speaker B: Couldn't be better, thank you.

To the untrained eye/ear

Meaning: Without special knowledge of the subject.

Example: To the untrained eye, it looks like a stack of old papers. But, believe it or not, this is the original manuscript of my first book.

Tough act to follow

Meaning: Someone or something so successful, exemplary, or effective that it overshadows anything that follows.

Example: John was a tough act to follow - a Nobel laureate with 40 years of experience in the field; Finding a replacement for my colleague Dan will be a tough act to follow.

To your heart's content

Meaning: As long as you wish; as much as you want.

Example: You can circle Paris to your heart's content; His wife let him eat and drink to his heart's content.

Treat/handle with kid gloves

Meaning: To treat someone/something very gently and carefully; be extremely polite and kind.

Example: She needs to be handled with kid gloves; We must treat the situation with kid gloves.

Trouble is brewing (or "something is brewing")

Meaning: A dangerous or difficult situation is developing.

Example: The informant made it clear that something was brewing and that you and your family were in great danger.

True to form

Meaning: Behaving in expected or predictable manner; as usual.

Example: True to form, Rita and Sam are late again; True to form, John asked to borrow some more money; True to form, she missed the flight.

Try your hand at something

Meaning: To do something for the first time.

Example: I've always wanted to try my hand at scuba diving.

Until all hours

Meaning: Very late; until a very late hour.

Example: We were up talking until all hours.

Until the dust settles

Meaning: Until the situation becomes calmer.

Example: You've caused a lot of trouble, and we'll have to leave town until the dust settles.

Walk with a spring in your step

Meaning: Walk energetically and happily.

Example: As Rita walked into the school that morning, there was a spring in her step.

Water under the bridge

Meaning: Something that happened a long time ago and doesn't bother you anymore.

Example: I forgive you, my dear friend! And that quarrel is just water under the bridge!

When push comes to shove

Meaning: When a situation becomes critical and you need to act; when a decision needs to be made; when something can no longer be ignored.

Example: Only Bella was there to help me when push came to shove.

With flying colours

Meaning: Successfully.

Example: He passed his college entrance exam with flying colours.

With one accord

Meaning: All together; in full agreement; at the same time.

Example: With one accord they left the room; We made the decision with one accord.

Without a hitch (or "with no hitches")

Meaning: Smoothly, easily, without any difficulties or problems.

Example: The parade went off without a hitch; The knee surgery went without a hitch.

Worth your while

Meaning: Something that is worth your attention/time and you can gain some benefit or advantage from it.

Dialogue example:

Speaker A: Is it really worth your while to keep looking for your grandmother's necklace?

Speaker B: Yes, that necklace is a family heirloom.

Printed in Great Britain
by Amazon

47307352R00040